D1440786

"LIKE NO OTHER GAME...LIKE REINVENTING THE WHEEL..."

R.S., Abidjan, Cote D'Ivoire, Africa.

"DOMINOS CAN COME OUT OF THE CLOSET NOW!"

L.A., Stanford, California, U.S.A.

"I'M TOTALLY HOOKED....IT'S NOT JUST FOR KIDS ANYMORE!"

J.M., Brooklyn, New York, U.S.A.

"READ THIS BOOK...INTERNATIONAL DOMINOS IS THE GAME OF THE 90'S!"

M.V. Salerno, Italy

"INTERNATIONAL DOMINOS" IS THE NEW FAMILY GAME IN OUR HOME, THANK YOU!

K.A. Woodstock, Vermont, U.S.A.

Published by
AVID PRESS
P.O. Box 158
Rosendale, NY 12472

International Dominos

By John Anderson and Jose Varuzza
Illustrated by Nick Driano
Cover by Greg McDermont

For Jessie, Jarett and Katie;
For dear friends and avid players;

With special thanks to Wally Sharp

TABLE OF CONTENTS

INTRODUCTION

It is surprising the number of people who are familiar with the game of dominos, who perhaps played with them as a child, and yet have no idea how exciting, challenging and enjoyable the game can be when played correctly. (Yes, there is more to it than setting them up and knocking them down.)

International Dominos is enjoyed throughout the world, from China, where many believe the game originated, to Europe. In South America and Central America the game has been played for many years, and now in the United States its popularity is growing tremendously.

While there are several regional variations, this book will guide you through the finer points of the actual game as it is played in most of the world, and enable you to play at a competent level anywhere.

The purpose of this book is to introduce you to this wonderful pastime and to provide a standardized reference guide to International Dominos.

The first pages contain all you need to know to start playing. The rest of the book will expand your abilities and show you some of the strategies and subtleties of the game.

International Dominos is a perfect blend of luck and skill. You needn't be a genius to play; however, the strategies and thinking involved will sustain your interest and enjoyment of the game. Drawing good tiles certainly makes it easier, but knowing what to do with them and how to interact with your partner is the key to the game.

The accompanying dominos set is a professional set complete with a convenient travel case.

Welcome to world class DOMINOS

PART I: THE BASICS

1.1 International Dominos

International Dominos is played by four players, two on each team. (The play of the game is the same for two or three players. For these variations, see the appendix.) Partners sit opposite one another. They are not allowed to communicate with other players in any way that could affect the fairness or the play of the game. Reasonable time is allowed for each player to consider which tile he or she wishes to play. Trying to determine what tiles your partner has, by the way he plays (we'll use ''he'' for the sake of simplicity), is very important. The successful inter-action of partners in the play of tiles can lead to great victories.

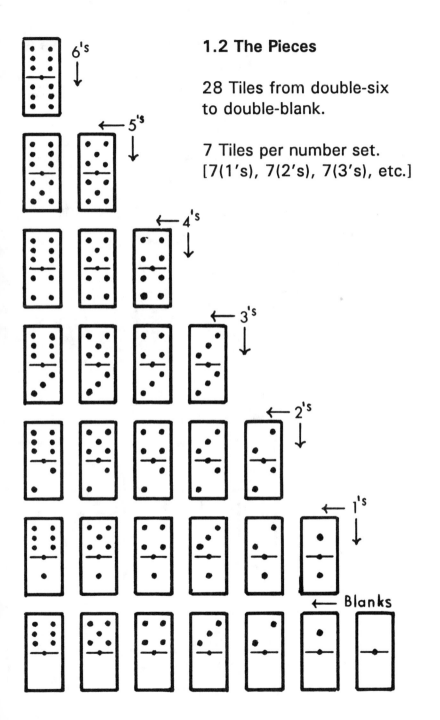

1.2 The Pieces

28 Tiles from double-six to double-blank.

7 Tiles per number set.
[7(1's), 7(2's), 7(3's), etc.]

6's

← 5's

← 4's

← 3's

← 2's

← 1's

← Blanks

9

Dominos are played so that the end of one tile is placed against the matching end of another tile.

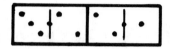

Doubles are always played crosswise, and the sides are played to, as illustrated.

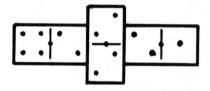

Ends of tiles, other than doubles, may also be placed against any of the three sides of a matching end.

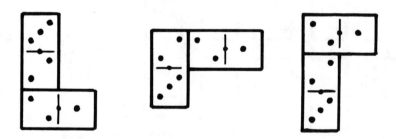

The following notation is used in the text to describe individual tiles; (6-6), (6-5), (6-4), (6-3), etc. The number under consideration for play is listed first.

1.3 Object of the Game

The object of the game is to match one end of a tile from your hand with an open end of the Dominos in play, and to be the first player to play all of your tiles. This is called "going out" and ends that particular hand or round.

The team which has one player "go out" collects the points (one point per spot) on the other team's unplayed tiles. To win a hand, it is necessary for only one of the partners to go out. His teammate's tiles are disregarded at this point and only the unplayed tiles of the team who lost the round are tallied. (One exception to this is explained in the section called "Locking a Hand"). Subsequent hands are played and the first team to reach 100 points wins the game.

1.4 Beginning a Hand

To begin a hand, place all of the dominos face down on the table. Mix them thoroughly by placing your hands flat on top of groups of tiles, and with light pressure, move them around and around. It takes only ten to fifteen seconds to mix the dominos well. The mixing pins in the center of each tile facilitate the process.

Often, a final, gentle push of the group of tiles is given to signal an end to the mixing as the tiles gently bounce off each other and settle in the middle of the table.

Each player then draws seven tiles and sets them up or holds them so that no other player can see the faces of the tiles. For the first hand of a game, any player, and often several, can mix the dominos. Each player then selects his seven tiles for that hand.

In subsequent hands, the player who started the play of one hand will be the player who mixes the tiles for the next hand. After mixing, he will allow the other three players to select their tiles before taking the last seven tiles for his own hand. The player to his left begins play of this round and will mix the next round and so forth.

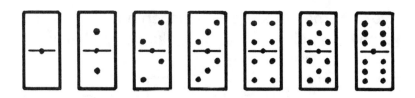

1.5 Drawing Five Doubles

If any player has drawn five or more doubles in one hand, the hand is thrown in and all of the tiles are remixed. Players again choose their hands as if the five-double round had not occurred. The same mixer will remix this round and the player to his left will begin the play.

1.6 Beginning the First Hand

For the first hand of a game, play is always begun by the player who has the DOUBLE-SIX. The player places the tile face up in the middle of the table.

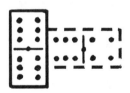

The player to his left plays next. He may play any tile that has a (6) on it to either side of the double-six. For example, the (6-4). Play continues in a clockwise rotation and the third player may now play either a tile with a (6) on it to the other side of the double-six, or play

13

a tile that matches the other open end of play, in the example just given, a (4). See illustration below.

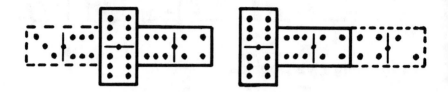

Each player always has a choice of two ends on which to play a matching tile from his hand. There is always ONLY TWO ENDS to play on.

Doubles are placed crosswise to adjoining tiles only so that their position is easily recognized. This facilitates the counting of sets of tiles that have been played. (More on this later when Strategies are discussed).

Non-doubles may be played end to end or to the left or right as illustrated in the **Introduction to the Pieces**. Thus, the dominos in play may turn corners and the two open ends remain accessible to play.

Play continues clockwise with each player taking a turn to play one tile. If a player has a tile that matches either of the open ends of the play, he MUST play it. If he has more than one tile that matches either of the open ends of play, he may select the tile of his choice to play. If he has no tiles that match the open ends of play, he passes his turn by saying "PASS", or by knocking twice on the table with his knuckles.

14

The turn passes to the next player in rotation and play continues until one player "goes out". The points are then tallied and the tiles are turned face down to be mixed for the next round.

As explained under mixing, the person who started the round just completed will mix the tiles for the next round, and the player to his left will begin the play. Hence the tiles will be mixed in round two by the player who started round one with the double-six. He will receive the last seven tiles after the other players have drawn theirs. Play for this new round is begun by the player to the left of the mixer.

When it is your turn to play, you must make a play if you have a playable tile. You may pass only if you have no playable tiles.

If a misplay occurs, for example a player plays a tile that he had passed on previously, the hand is thrown in, remixed and replayed. At the option of the players, penalties may be added to the scoring to prevent abuse of this rule.

1.7 Subsequent Rounds

Round one was started with the double-six. Round two and all subsequent rounds in a single game will begin with ANY double the starter may have in his hand. If he has several doubles he may select any one of them to begin the play. If he has one double, he MUST start with it. If he has no doubles, he may start with any of the seven tiles he holds. Play continues as in round one until one player goes out.

1.8 Locked Hand

A round is considered "locked" when none of the players can play to either end; in other words, when all four players consecutively pass. If this happens, the unplayed tiles on each team are tallied and the team with the lower tally wins the hand. They then receive ALL of the points remaining in the other team's two hands.

If both team's tally is the same, then the round is a tie and no scoring occurs. A new round is mixed and played and designation of the mixer and starter is rotated clockwise just as if the round had been a scoring round. In other words, if player two started the round that ended in a tie, then he will mix and player three will start the new round.

The game can be locked unintentionally because players may be forced to play tiles that create the locking pattern. More often, the lock is intentional and sometimes strived for.

In the example below, the player whose turn it is holds the (2-1), which is the last tile with a (1) on it remaining available for play. (For this example, we are presuming that the other six tiles with a (1) on them have been played). He has the choice of playing the (2-1) on either end since one open end is a (2) and the other open end is a (1).

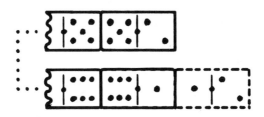

If he plays the (1) to the (1), then both open ends will be (2's) and play will continue since there are more (2's) available for playing. If however, the player thinks that his partner and he are holding lower points in their hands than their opponents, then he will play the (2-1) to the (2) end of the play. Both open ends will now be (1's) and no one will be able to play on them (see below). The hand is locked and points are tallied as previously explained.

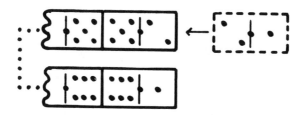

The same situation occurs if, in the example just cited, besides the (2-1), the double-one is still available for play. If the player plays the (2-1) so as to lock the game, it will still be effective because the only possible remaining play is for the double-one to come out. The lock is then secured as four passes will ensue.

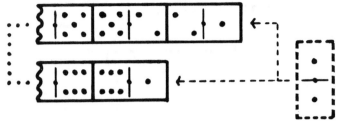

Note that if the (2-1) were played the other way, so that both ends became (2's), the person holding the double-one would never be able to play it. This is referred to as being "locked out" or "eating a double". More on this in the next section on doubles.

NOTE: Some strategies and examples may at first seem complex, but they will become clear as you play the game.

PART II STRATEGIES

2.1 Counting Tiles

Counting tiles is not a strategy but rather the key to all strategies. It is only by counting tiles that you can ascertain what has and has not been played. You must count tiles to avoid or work towards a lock. You must count tiles to work towards gaining control of the play. It is to facilitate counting that doubles are placed crosswise, enabling one to locate them at a glance. Counting tiles simply means keeping track of how many tiles of each set of seven have been played. This enables you to determine which tiles are outstanding, and from this you can choose your best options for playing.

2.2 Doubles

The doubles have advantages and disadvantages. Holding a lot of doubles limits the versatility and options for playing a hand. That is why drawing five doubles allows one to throw in the hand for remixing. Drawing four doubles has to be one of the least favorable hands to play. In less extreme situations, having a couple of doubles can add dimension to your hand. If you are strong in any particular set of tiles, leading the double should pull into play two more tiles of that set.

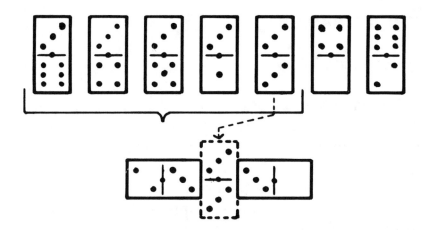

For example, of the seven (3's), if you have five of them including the double, leading with the double-three can pull out the remaining two (3's), leaving you with the last four of the unplayed (3's) in your hand. This greatly enhances your chances of taking control of the play.

Once you play one of them so that an open end has a (3) showing, you are the only player who can play to it. If you can play so that both open ends become (3's), you will soon be out. This is your introduction to strategies for controlling the ends.

When four numbers of a set have been played and you hold the last two and the double, it can assure you of a round of play.

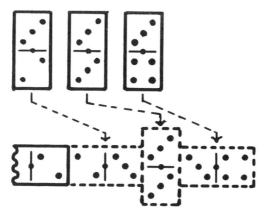

If four (3's) have been played and you hold the (2-3), (3-3), and (4-3), and the play comes to you with either a (2) or a (4) open on one of the ends, you can take control of that end. As illustrated above, if the end has a (2) showing, then you can play the (2-3) and next turn the (3-3) and finally go out with the (3-4).

Even more dramatically, in the example just given, if the play comes to you with a (2) and a (4) on the open ends, and if six (2's) have been played, then your (2-3) controls one of the ends already.

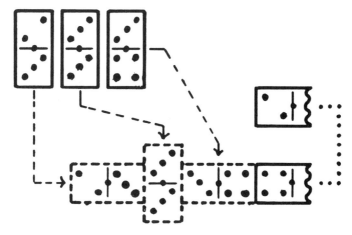

Your play should then be to the other end with your (4-3), taking control of the round. After the other players all pass, you will play the (3-3), forcing another three passes. You will then go out with a lock with the (3-2) played on either end. This is your introduction to strategies which emphasize the importance of counting tiles and knowing how many of each set of numbers are waiting to be played. (Although you may want to savor your victory, it is not necessary to wait for the other players to pass before playing out your tiles when you have taken total control of a round. Players are known to slam them down rather exuberantly).

2.3 Strong vs. Weak Double

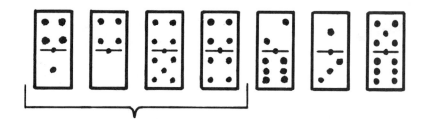

A strong double is one of several tiles in any number set that you hold.

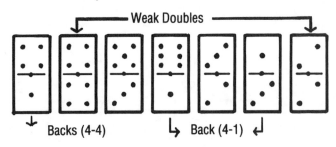

Backs (4-4)   Back (4-1)

22

A weak double is one by itself or with only one other of the same number set. It is generally better to play a weak double at an early opportunity. One must always be alert to the danger of having a weak double "locked out" as the other six tiles of that set pair up in the play. This leaves you with no place to play the double. (This is when you hope your partner can go out).

Holding a backer for the double, another tile of the same set, helps to avert this risk. Sometimes it is necessary to back it twice. For example, a (4-1) backs the (4-4), and a (1-anything) backs the (4-1). By holding an extra (1) you are not forced to play the (4-1) tile and it can continue to back the (4-4). See previous illustration.

There are rare instances when you can intentionally lock out your own double because this would enable your partner to play his last tile and go out.

2.4 Locking Out a Double

One of the strategies with great satisfaction potential is to play to lock out an opponent's double. Locking out a small double (such as the (1-1) or the (2-2)) prevents that player from going out. Locking out a large double, particularly the (6-6), adds insult to injury.

An example of this strategy is when player one starts with a non-double and you are player four holding several (6's) in your hand. You know that the double-six must be in your partner's hand or player three's hand because you don't have it, and player one didn't start with a double.

Player one ⟶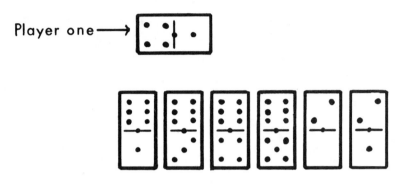

Player four's hand

You should play (6's) at early opportunities. If your partner has the double-six, he will get a chance to "dump it". If he doesn't, he has the chance to play on your (6) and close it off from player three. Either way, you are pushing your strong (6's) out, and if the distribution is favorable, possibly sticking the opponent with a twelve point tile in his hand.

Note that if one player has no doubles to lead, then it's very possible that one of the other players has a four-double, tough hand to try to play. It is definite that one of the other players holds at least three doubles. These simple observations will help you try to determine what the other players hold in their hands and thus what the lead player holds also.

The same type of situation as the last example occurs if you have no doubles and start the play with a (6-anything) because you are strong in (6's). If the next player passes, your partner knows to play the double-six if he has it. If he doesn't have it, he knows that it must be in player four's hand because you started with no double and player two passed. His job then, is to close the (6) end and try to lock out the double-six.

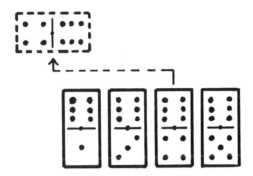

If, in this example, you start with the (6-4) and player two plays on the (4) end, the same scenario is probably true although not necessarily. Unless player two is also strong in (6's), it is most likely that he would play the double-six in this situation if he had it.

These are examples of strategies gained from the strength of information. One illustrates the informative power of a pass. The other shows the importance of watching what has not been played as well as what has been played.

2.5 Observing the Play

If a player appears to be trying to avoid playing on a particular number, he is likely to be weak or out of that number, or the very opposite. He may be very strong in that number and waiting for others to play tiles of that set which would strengthen his hand. Careful observation of what is and is not played can help you discern which possibility is more likely and help you learn more about the make-up of the other players hands.

If a player is seemingly trying to push a certain number, then he is probably very strong in that set. It would then be wise for his opponents to try and hold onto a tile from that set to prevent him from taking control. One can even go into a counter strategy by trying to force the player to play from his strength.

If, for example, player two is strong in (3's) and seemingly pushing them, then he is going to have less of some other numbers. If you are player one and do not play on an open (3) end, but rather play tiles on the other end, of which many are already in play, or of which you are strong, you increase the likelihood that player two will have to play to the (3) end. This will take away from his strength. The key to the play is to recognize strengths and weaknesses and look for opportunities to exploit them.

2.6 Observing Passes

A player conveys more information when he passes than with any other move. It is extremely important to remember which players pass and on what numbers they passed. (Players are not allowed to write any of this information down). This information is definite and is your strongest indication of what the other players hold. You gain a tempo each time you can force opponents to pass, and you are one tile closer to going out.

If a player passes on (2's) and (4's), you will do well to try to play those numbers to him again. If both ends are (2's) or (4's), he will pass again. Even if only one end has a (2) or a (4), he will be limited to the other end to play on. His partner will also be constrained in his play because he must try not to give you opportunities to play a (2) or a (4) to the passer.

When a player passes, his partner should give consideration to which tile might allow the passer an

27

opportunity to play.

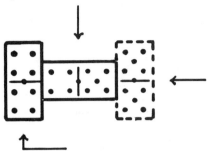

If player one leads the (4-4), player two passes and player three plays the (4-5), player four should only play on the open (5) if he has a tile that prevents player one from making both ends (4's), because that would force player two to pass again. The (5-5) would acheive this because the (5-4) was just played.

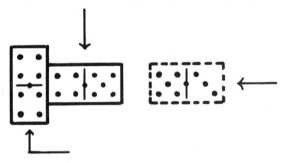

The (5) with any other number would achieve this if player four held the (4) with that same number, because player one obviously couldn't then play it. Any play on the (4) end would prevent the ends from showing (4's) to the passer.

If you are player four, it may be preferable to make a safe play to the (5) end. If the lead was a strong double-four, then you might force player one to play another (4) and thus dilute the strength of his remaining (4's). If it was not a strong double being led, then either you or player three have the strong (4's), because player two has none. If it is player three, then your playing the (5) end has the same effect of possibly forcing him to play another (4) and diluting his strength. If you are strong in (4's), then obviously, playing the (5) end may pull out another (4) and enhance the strength of your (4's).

It's to your advantage to try to make other players play tiles that may not be their first choice. Anytime you make a player play a tile that you like, he is prevented from playing a tile that he might prefer. This works equally against you, and is why you try to help your partner avoid passing, and try to stay away from your opponents strengths.

It should be obvious that if the play is such that you can take full control of it and see your way to going out, then it is of no concern that your partner is passing a lot.

2.7 Options vs. Control

One method of avoiding passing your own turn is to look for a balance in your hand that leaves you as many options to play as possible. If the play comes to you with a (4) and a (2) on the ends and if you hold two (4's) but only one (2), then it may be better to play one of the (4's).

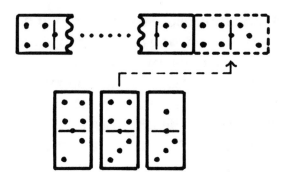

If the play comes to you with (4's) on each end and you hold the (4-2), (4-3), and (3-1), then it may be better to play the (4-3) because you have another (3). Your remaining tiles allow you four options of play; on a (1), (2), (3), or (4). If you had played the (4-2), you would have only three options of play remaining; on a (1), (3), or (4).

Please note that these strategies are not rules set in stone. In the example just given, the weaker alternative, playing the (4-2), could in some cases be the better play because it would leave you with two (3's).

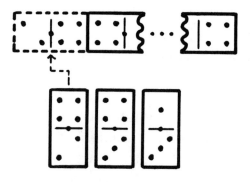

If these were the last (3's), then you would have an opportunity to take control of an end if a (1) or a (4) is played to you. The correct play depends on the particular tiles held in relation to those already played.

Generally, it's better to favor more options at the beginning of a hand and to wait to see how the play is unfolding before trying to decide whether to play towards taking control of a particular number set.

2.8 The Back Door

Maximizing your options to play increases your chances to go out. One of the ways to play for this we call the ''backdoor'' or ''playing away from yourself''. This is the practice of playing a tile that is not of your strongest set, but that may pull out from another player a tile of your strongest set. For example, if you are strong in (6's) and (3's) but don't have the (6-3), then pushing the (3's) may pull out the (6-3). This further enhances the strength of your (6's).

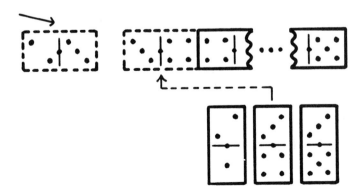

If five (2's) have been played and you hold the (2-1) plus a couple of (3's), and someone else holds the (3-2), then pushing the (3's) will pull out the (3-2) and give you control of that end because your (2-1) is now the last (2). Generally, it is better to try and get other players to play tiles of your strong set. This leaves your tiles intact and their strength enhanced. (See previous illustration)

If you have four (6's) and someone else plays an end to show a (6), then try to avoid that end because it may pull out the double-six and the other (6), leaving you with control of the last four (6's).

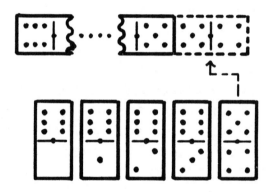

If you have the four (6's) shown above, it would normally take play of two of your (6's) to pull out the others, which would leave you with the last two (6's). This is good, but obviously not as strong as holding the last four (6's). Please note, though, that there would be no joy holding those last four (6's) if the opponents managed to lock the game at this point. Your decision to hold back or to push your tiles has to be based on the play of that particular hand.

2.9 A Final Point

This book has emphasized the importance of recognizing the strengths and weaknesses of a hand. It has also indicated various strategies to play with these strengths and weaknesses. One final point to emphasize is that the strength of a hand is dependent also on the play of that particular round. It is possible to have a seemingly strong hand and to be left out of sync with the play. We have frequently seen hands with four and sometimes five of a number set unable to take control of the play. Imagine that player's consternation as he watches the play pass him by.

You can see now that there is no clear path to victory. This book can not say ''play such and such and you will win''. The game would not be so incredibly interesting if this were the case. The game is a balance and interaction of many factors. These include the draw, the play, the partners, the opponents, luck, and skill.

Each hand begins with many possible choices and outcomes. The particular outcome is determined by the above factors.

Work through the examples in this book so that you can recognize them in the actual play. Play some open hands (all tiles visible to all players) so that you can see and discuss possible plays. Then start playing International Dominos often. Your skill and enjoyment will grow the more you play. If the fun and challenge of International Dominos sometimes seems addictive .... well, you're welcome!

Part III Appendix

3.1 Variation for Two or Three Players.

a. Mix tiles.

b. Each player picks seven tiles, leaving the extras face down.

c. Player holding the highest double starts the game. If no doubles are held, the player with the highest non-double will start. (For example, the (6-5), or (6-4), or (6-3), etc.) In subsequent hands, the rules for mixing and starting are the same as for four players.

d. Play is the same as with four players.

e. If a player can not make a play, he picks ONE TILE from the extras and plays it if possible. If he can't play it, he passes that turn. (If there are no extra tiles to pick from at any point in the game, then the player simply passes that turn.)

f. Play continues until one player goes out or locks the hand. A hand is not locked if any possibility of play exists in the extra tiles. Simply counting to see if all seven tiles are played will determine if the lock is valid.

g. For TWO players, score the same as for four players. (The first player to reach 100 points wins the game).

h. For THREE players, tally the points in each player's

hand and score the total under their individual columns. The person who goes out or who has the lowest tally in a lock scores zero under his name. (A three way tie in a lock scores zero for each player. A two way tie scores zero for both players if the third player's tally is higher. It scores against both players if the third player's tally is lower.) When one of the three players reaches 100 points, the player with the lowest score wins the game.

i. Our preferred variation for three players has each player draw nine tiles. One tile is thus left face down on the table, unknown to the players and out of the play during the hand. Play commences and is scored as in ''h'', above.

We think that these variations for two or three players are better than any other dominos variations we have seen. However, (short of kidnapping) we would recommend finding or teaching other players so that you have the full complement of four players for your game of International Dominos.

3.2 Spinning the Tiles

With LIGHT pressure from your thumb on the center of a tile, and by pulling your index or middle finger across the corner of the tile (in a movement similar to snapping your finger), you can set the tile spinning on its pin.

It is even possible to set more than one tile spinning at the same time. Since so many players spin tiles, we provide you with this brief description here. At best, this useless manuever may make you appear like an experienced player, or it may simply keep your hands busy and moderate your intake of snacks.

3.3 Scoring Tip

Scoring is simply tallied in a column for each team. A helpful tip is to put the initials of the starter by each hand so that you can easily determine whose turn it is to mix, and who is to start the next round. Be sure to note any unscored round where a lock ended in a tie.

3.4 Sample Games

Note: These examples were taken from actual games that we observed. The variations dramatically show the outcome of different choices in the play.

Game I-A

Player one: (1-5) (2-5) (3-5) (5-5) (0-0) (4-4) (6-6)
Player two: (1-3) (1-0) (1-2) (0-3) (0-4) (2-6) (4-6)
Player Three: (0-5) (1-1) (1-4) (1-6) (2-2) (3-4) (5-6)
Player four: (0-2) (3-2) (3-3) (3-6) (0-6) (4-2) (4-5)

Player 1	Player 2	Player 3	Player 4
	Leads (1-0)	(0-5)	(5-4)
(4-4)	(4-0)	(1-1)	(0-2)
(1-5)	(2-6)	(6-1)	pass
(5-5)	(1-3)	(3-4)	(4-2)
(2-5)	pass	(5-6)	(6-3)
(3-5)! locks!			

Player 1 and 3 get 33 points from player 2 and 4. Player 1 has four doubles but the strength of his four (5's) prevail.

Game I-B

Player 1	Player 2	Player 3	Player 4
	Leads (1-0)	(1-1)	(0-2)
(2-5)	(1-2)	(5-6)?	(6-3)!
(3-5)	(2-6)	(5-0)	(6-0)!
(0-0)	(0-4)	(4-1)	pass
(1-5)	(0-3)	(3-4)	(5-4)!!
(4-4)	(4-6)	(6-1)	(4-2)
pass	(1-3) out.		

Players 2 and 4 get 26 points from players 1 and 3.
Same hand, different play, different ending.

(5-6)? - The (2-2) is better. See game I-C
(6-3) and (6-0)! - This play closes (6) and prevents
             play of the (6-6).
(5-4)!! - Closes (5) and locks out (5-5).

39

Game I-C

Player 1	Player 2	Player 3	Player 4
	Leads (1-0)	(1-1)	(0-2)
(2-5)	(1-2)	(2-2)	(5-4)
(4-4)	(2-6)	(6-5)!	(2-3)
(3-5)!!	pass	(5-0)	(0-6)
(6-6)	(6-2)	pass	(2-4)
(5-5)*	(4-0)	pass	pass
(0-0)	(0-3)	(3-4)	pass
(5-1) out.			

Players 1 and 3 get 19 points from players 2 and 4.

(6-5)! - Player 2 has no doubles (He led the (1-0)). Player 4 did not play (5-5) on last turn. The (6-5) thus pushes (5's) to player 1.

(3-5)!! - Takes control with his (5's).

(5-5)* - Coasting while looking to play (0-0) or an opportunity to lock the hand with (1-5).

Game II

Player one: (0-0) (0-3) (4-3) (4-4) (6-3) (6-5) (5-5)
Player two: (0-2) (2-2) (3-2) (6-2) (5-2) (5-1) (1-1)
Player three: (6-6) (6-1) (0-1) (2-4) (5-4) (5-3) (3-3)
Player four: (2-1) (3-1) (4-1) (4-0) (5-0) (6-0) (6-4)

Player 1	Player 2	Player 3	Player 4
Leads (5-5)	(5-2)!	(2-4)	(4-6)
(5-6)	(6-2)!	(6-6)	(6-0)
(0-3)	(3-2)!	pass	(2-1)
pass	(1-1)	(1-6)	pass
(6-3)	(2-2)*	(3-3)	(3-1)
pass	(1-5)	(5-4)	(4-1)!
pass	(0-2) out.		

Player 2 and 4 get 24 points from players 1 and 3.

(5-2)! (6-2)! (3-2)! - pushing out other (2's) and
    taking control.
(2-2)* - Coasting while looking to play (5-1) or to
    lock with (0-2)
(4-1)! - Forces another pass.

41

Game III-A

Player one: (4-4) (1-4) (3-4) (1-3) (6-5) (5-0) (2-2)
Player two: (0-6) (0-0) (0-1) (1-1) (6-1) (6-2) (3-2)
Player three: (2-0) (2-5) (2-4) (5-4) (6-4) (6-3) (3-3)
Player four: (5-5) (3-5) (1-5) (1-2) (0-4) (0-3) (6-6)

Player 1	Player 2	Player 3	Player 4
	Leads (1-1)	pass	(1-5)
(1-4)!	pass	(5-4)!!	(4-0)
(0-5)!!	pass	(5-2)	(2-1)
(4-4)	(1-0)	(0-2)	pass
(2-2)	(2-6)	(6-4)!!	pass
(4-3)	(3-2)	(2-4) lock.	

Player 1 and 3 get 46 points from players 2 and 4.

(1-4)! - Allows partner to play.
(5-4)!! - Pushes (4's).
(0-5)!! - Forces another pass.
(6-4)!! - Asserts strong (4's) - see Game III-B

Game III-B

The same as Game III-A up to turn where player three's (6-4)!! takes control. Instead of the (6-4), if player three plays the (6-3):

Player 1	Player 2	Player 3	Player 4
		(6-3)??	(3-0)
(4-3)	(3-2)	(2-4)	pass
pass	(0-0)	(4-6)	(6-6)
(6-5)	(0-6)	pass	(5-5)
pass	(6-1) out.		

Players 1 and 3 lose ten points to players 2 and 4.

(6-3)?? - Failure to assert strong (4's) causes a 10 point loss versus the 46 point win in Game III-A.

3.5 MILO

International Dominos, as presented in this book, is by far the most popular game. It is this game that is referred to around the world when people say "Dominos". The play is virtually the same in every country with some very minor variations.

Milo, the most fascinating variation, is played in parts of Africa and Indonesia. Milo is played exactly the same as International Dominos with four people playing in two partnerships. The difference is in the scoring.

When one player "goes out", his team wins one point for that hand. Spots are counted only to determine which team wins the one point when a hand is locked. The first team to win five points wins that game. If a player "goes out" with a tile that makes the two ends of the play show the same number, (for example, a player "goes out" with a tile that results in a 4 showing on each end of the tiles in play), this is a "Milo" and scores double, or two points, for that team.

What is fascinating about this variation is that all tiles are thus equal. A double six counts no more against a player than a double blank, so there is no urgency to try and unload the higher numbered tiles when it appears that the opponents may be about to go out.

3.6 Other Dominos Games

There are many other games that can be played with Dominos tiles. Most of these are of no interest or popular appeal, except for the following two regional U.S. games.

Muggins and Company

Predominantly on the west coast, there is a set of Dominos variations where points are scored when the open ends of play add up to an exact multiple of five: one point if they add up to five, two points if they add up to ten, three points if they add up to fifteen, etc. Rather than just two open ends of play, tiles can be played on all sides of each double creating many new open ends of play. This creates many possible exact multiples of five for scoring. When a player goes out, this player receives one point for each multiple of five spots on the tiles remaining in his opponents' hands.

With two players, each player begins with seven tiles. Each begins with six tiles when there are three players, and five tiles when there are four players. The remaining tiles are set aside as the "boneyard". The player with the highest double begins the play. Each player in turn plays one tile. If a player does not hold a playable tile, he must pick tiles from the boneyard until he can make a play. If there are no tiles in the boneyard, he must pass. Play continues until one player goes out. If the play should become locked, the player with the least spots left in his hand is the winner. He will subtract the sum of the spots on his unplayed tiles from the sum of his opponents' spots and receive one point for each multiple of five in the total.

Forty-Two

Found mostly in the Texas area and in the South, Forty-Two is for four players on two teams. The tiles are played more like cards than like Dominos, with a trump suit, bidding, and royals.

Each player picks a tile and the highest tile holder will bid first. All tiles are mixed and each player draws seven. Each player will pass or make a bid based on how many points he thinks his team will win in the play. The minimum bid is thirty of a possible forty-two points which consist of the following:

(1) One point for each of seven possible tricks to be won in the play.

(2) Five points for winning the royal 4-1, 3-2, or 5-0 in the play.

(3) Ten points for winning the royal 5-5, or 6-4 in the play.

The highest bidder leads a tile and declares which of the number sets on the tile will be trump for that hand. Each player plays in turn and must follow suit (play a tile with the same number set as was led). The highest tile played in the suit that was led wins the trick.

The winner of a trick leads for the next trick. Unless he leads trump, the suit to be followed is the higher of the number sets on the lead tile. For example, leading a 3-1 makes 3's the suit led unless 1's are trump.

A player must follow suit. If he has none of the suit led, he may play a trump or play any other tile. Tricks are won by the highest tile in the suit that was led unless someone has played trump. Then, the highest trump played wins.

The winner of a trick turns the tiles face down in front of him. After seven tricks, each team counts their points as listed above. If the team that won the bid makes or exceeds their bid, they score the amount of the bid plus the amount that they have won in the play. If they don't make their bid, then the opponents score the amount of the bid plus the amount that the opponents won in the play. Play continues until one team reaches 150 or other agreed upon number.

THE END

"The end" of this book, but the beginning of the enjoyment of International Dominos. If Bridge is the most perfect of all the possible card games, then International Dominos is the most perfect and widely played game of Dominos. We are happy to be a major part of the discovery by North Americans of this classic game, and we are grateful for all the thank you mail that we receive. Although International Dominos is played very seriously and sometimes with wagering, it is equally enjoyable as a parlor game with family and friends.

After playing a few games, refer back to the strategy sections and the sample games in this book. You will begin to discover the subtleties that make International Dominos a variable and versatile pastime that produces new surprises every time.

We have played International Dominos in most of the world; in homes, in cafes, on crates in a small village or tables in a city square. We have played when there was no language in common with the other players. Good people, good food and drink, good play and great smiles, this is the language appreciated all over the world: International Dominos!